TRAMWAY

"Lee Moor No.2", with 17 empty wagons which she had brought from the top of the Cann Wood Incline, approaches Torycombe Level Crossing on August 18th 1939.
(Photograph - E.R. Shepherd)

All rights reserved. No part of this publication may be reproduced, stored in a retrieval system, or transmitted in any form or by any means, electronic, mechanical, photocopying, or recording or otherwise, without the prior permission of the copyright holder.

Written by Bryan Gibson

Printed by Design and Print, Plympton

© Published by the Plymouth Railway Circle. 1993

ISBN 0 9521139 0 2

Bibliography

Lee Moor Tramway (Meade-King 1961)

The Lee Moor Tramway (Hall 1963)

The Plymouth and Dartmoor Railway (Kendall 1968)

Railway Magazine (1908, 1909, 1934, 1941, 1946 and 1969)

Lee Moor Tramway Preservation Society Newsletters

Plymouth Railway Circle Magazines and Minute Books

Acknowledgements

Larry Crosier, Maurice Dart, Eric Shepherd, Roy Taylor and David Tozer of the erstwhile Lee Moor Tramway Preservation Society. Ray Coxon, Frank Jones, Alan Jackson and Dick Riley.

Cover Photograph

A train of sand from Marsh Mills to Maddock's Concrete Works, crosses the London - Penzance main line at Laira on June 7th, 1950. (R.T. Coxon)

THE LEE MOOR TRAMWAY

The foot of the Torycombe Incline, showing the cable rollers.
(Photograph - F.H.C. Casbourn, courtesy of the Stephenson Locomotive Society)

Foreword

China-clay is one the country's most important raw materials. It has been mined around St. Austell in Cornwall and in the Lee Moor area near Plymouth since 1755 and 1835 respectively. The clay is the product of decomposed granite and has many uses in modern life; its primary application is in the manufacture of high quality paper, but it is also a constituent in the production of porcelain, pharmaceuticals and cosmetics. The Devon and Cornwall deposits are amongst the largest in the world and, because of its high quality, the refined product is one of the country's most valued exports.

The area around St. Austell is outside the scope of this publication and has been comprehensively covered in two excellent volumes, "The Newquay Branch and its Branches" and "An Illustrated History of West Country China Clay Trains", both by noted railway author John Vaughan. This booklet relates the history of the tramway which was built to convey the china-clay from Lee Moor to the port of Plymouth. Its construction was influenced by the presence of the Plymouth & Dartmoor Railway, which had been in use before a railway to Lee Moor was considered, and paragraphs about it are relevant.

Water tank wagons, used to increase the weight of trains descending the Torycombe Incline.
(Photograph - F.H.C. Casbourn, courtesy of the Stephenson Locomotive Society)

The Plymouth & Dartmoor Railway

This early enterprise was proposed by local landowner and Plymouth MP Sir Thomas Tyrwhitt as a means of linking Princetown to Plymouth, with a view to opening up Dartmoor for development. What we now know as Dartmoor Prison was built in 1809 to house French prisoners of war, but after the Napoleonic Wars and the departure of the last detainees in February 1816, the gaunt buildings stood empty. The effect on Princetown was profound and proposals to inject new life were urgently needed; using the prison to incarcerate convicted law-breakers was suggested at this time, but not undertaken until November 1850.

The Plymouth & Dartmoor Railway was a great innovation in its day; the use of wagons with flanged wheels running on cast-iron rails allowed horses to pull much greater payloads than would have been possible on the unmetalled roads of the day. The railway was laid to a gauge of 4'6" and was opened between a dock on the River Plym at Crabtree (near the present-day A38 junction at Marsh Mills) and Foggintor Quarries on September 26th, 1823.

Many reasons for a choice so close to the present day 4'8½" have been postulated, but at that time there was no such thing as "Standard Gauge". It should be remembered that railways were in their infancy in the early 1800's; the national railway map had yet to be drawn and the main line from London did not reach Plymouth until 1848. The Plymouth & Dartmoor pre-dated the 4'8½" Stockton & Darlington Railway by two years and it was another half-century before this eventual Standard Gauge found its way into Plymouth. In 1823, a round figure of 4½ft could well have been no more than an arbitrary but logical choice.

Navigation of the River Plym up to Crabtree was only possible at higher states of the tide and the dock was prone to silting, so in December 1825 the Plymouth & Dartmoor Railway was extended to Sutton Harbour, with a branch to Martin's Wharf on the River Plym. At the other end of the line, the final two miles from Foggintor Quarries to Princetown were opened some twelve months later.

"Lee Moor No.1" outside the engine shed in about 1900, when she still had her name painted on the saddle tank. With the crew are employees of the Truck Repair Shop.
(Photograph from the Lee Moor Tramway Preservation Society)

The railway never fulfilled Sir Thomas's aim of opening up Dartmoor to the degree that he had intended and the only traffic of any consequence was the granite won from the quarries around Foggintor, Swell Tor and Ingra Tor. The Johnson brothers, who worked the quarries, had a virtual stranglehold over the railway by dint of their financial involvement in the line's construction. The conveyance rates that they negotiated were so low that the Plymouth & Dartmoor was virtually their private railway.

The Cann Quarry Branch of the Plymouth & Dartmoor Railway

The Earl of Morley, whose family home was at Saltram, owned much of the land in the Plym Valley area and this was encroached upon by the route of the Plymouth & Dartmoor Railway. In return for the line's free passage, the Plymouth & Dartmoor had undertaken to provide a link to the Earl's blue slatestone quarry in Cann Wood, which had been worked since at least 1664. The Plymouth & Dartmoor passed within a quarter mile of the quarry, but having climbed all the way from Crabtree, was over 150ft. above it.

One of the options was an inclined plane, but in the event, a branch line was built to connect the south end of the Cann Quarry Canal at Marsh Mills with the Plymouth & Dartmoor line at Crabtree. This branch line opened during the winter of 1829/30 and in 1833 was diverted from the canal terminus and extended up the valley to Plym Bridge, along the canal's towpath and into the quarry; the canal was rendered redundant as a means of transport but survived for some years as a mill leat.

The Plympton Branch of the Plymouth & Dartmoor Railway

It had been known for some time that there were rich deposits of china-clay at Lee Moor, and Lord Morley, who had the mineral rights, leased these to J & W Phillips in September 1833. To take the china-clay from these new workings, another line was proposed, branching off the recently opened Cann Quarry line at Marsh Mills, along the north side of the present day Plymouth Road to within sight of St. Mary's Church in Plympton and then up the valley of the Tory Brook to Lee Moor; the first section from Marsh Mills to Plympton opened in 1834, just as extraction was starting at Lee Moor.

Construction from Plympton to the clay works was thwarted by the refusal of George Strode of Newnham to allow the railway to pass through his land and the line never reached Lee Moor by this route. This outcome was far from satisfactory, as the clay had to be brought down to Plympton by packhorse before it could be railed for the remainder of the journey into Plymouth.

"Lee Moor No.1", now wearing a cast nameplate, at Torycombe Level Crossing in about 1922.
(Photograph - F.H.C. Casbourn, courtesy of the Stephenson Locomotive Society)

The South Devon Railway

The main line from London had reached Totnes by way of the Great Western Railway, the Bristol & Exeter Railway and the South Devon Railway in July 1847. It was heading west by a difficult route which took it over the southern foothills of Dartmoor and the only feasible approach from high ground was down the Chaddle Wood gulley into Plympton. The terminus of the Plympton Branch of the Plymouth & Dartmoor Railway stood in the path of the new line and was sacrificed to give the South Devon Railway a clear run into Plymouth. It is unclear whether the Plympton Branch was truncated on the other side of the new South Devon Railway or closed in its entirety.

"Lee Moor No.2" alongside the "Dis" Mill at Torycombe in 1935. Fred Andrews is on the footplate and George Poynter is alongside the wagons.
(Photograph from the LGRP Collection, courtesy of the National Railway Museum, York)

The South Devon & Tavistock Railway

Another attempt at constructing a railway to Lee Moor was made in 1850 when John Andrew, a Plympton surveyor, prepared plans for a line from the Plymouth & Dartmoor Railway's Cann Quarry Branch at Plym Bridge. However any development of this idea was eclipsed by public interest in a railway to Tavistock; the South Devon sponsored South Devon & Tavistock Railway issued a prospectus in July 1852 to promote a 7'0¼" gauge line from Tavistock to a junction with the South Devon Railway's main line at Marsh Mills.

The proposed route was through Lord Morley's land in the Plym Valley and would have needed the trackbed of the Plymouth & Dartmoor Railway's Cann Quarry Branch. To secure his support, the South Devon & Tavistock Railway undertook to construct a branch to Lee Moor within six months of being given possession of the land. It was intended to build this branch to the same 4'6" gauge as the Cann Quarry Branch to permit through running, but the Earl was given the option to have it converted to 7'0¼" in due course. Ultimately, this would result in a line from Tavistock to Marsh Mills, using the trackbed of the Cann Quarry Branch south of Plym Bridge, and a branch to Lee Moor, both built to the 7'0¼" gauge.

The Construction of the Lee Moor Tramway

The formal contract to build the line was awarded to Messrs Hutchinson and Ritson on February 15th, 1853, but a start had already been made on earthworks in the previous September. The line was to be built under the direction of the South Devon & Tavistock Railway at a cost of £7,150 (about £350,000 in 1993 values) and opening was required by May 1st of the same year. Construction was completed twelve months later than contracted and trial working was under way in August 1854.

The Winding House at the top of Cann Wood Incline, looking towards Torycombe.
(Photograph - F.H.C. Casbourn, courtesy of the Stephenson Locomotive Society)

The line was very poorly built and the engineering works failed to reach the required specifications. The unsafe condition of the line was exposed by an incident on the Cann Wood Incline on October 4th, 1854 which resulted in temporary closure. The standard of construction must have been shoddy throughout; in addition to remedial work on Plym Bridge Viaduct, Truelove Bridge and Lower Leigh Viaduct, it was necessary to compact the earthworks and replace all the track. A 3" negative super elevation was found on the curve at the foot of the Torycombe Incline, but there must have been other deficiencies, as the incline was abandoned in favour of a new alignment, leaving the original line at the Plym Bridge end of Lee Moor Clay Works.

William Phillips at Lee Moor was frustrated by this débâcle, as the china-clay had to be taken down to the Cann Quarry line at Plym Bridge by packhorse, whilst the Lee Moor Tramway was being rebuilt. He saw no alternative but to undertake an independent survey of the standard of construction and take over the Tramway. An agreement dated June 5th, 1856 terminated the South Devon & Tavistock Railway's interest in the Tramway and Lord Morley and Phillips secured the right to work their china-clay traffic through to Plymouth as long as the 4'6" gauge remained. The South Devon Railway had purchased the Sutton Harbour Branch from the Plymouth & Dartmoor Railway in 1851 and laid 4'6" / 7'0¼" mixed-gauge track in 1857; the 4'6" gauge survived until 1869.

Rebuilding and Subsequent Developments

After the problems of 1854, the Tramway was rebuilt and opened again on September 24th, 1858. The Tavistock line was still incomplete and the Lee Moor Tramway traffic therefore used the Cann Quarry Branch and the Plymouth & Dartmoor "main line" below Crabtree to reach Plymouth. The Tramway traffic had exclusive use of the Cann Quarry Branch, as the quarry had closed in 1855, and exercised the Plymouth & Dartmoor Railway's right to cross the South Devon main line at Laira.

This caused a problem for the promoters of the new Tavistock line, as the unexpected continued presence of the Cann Quarry Branch prevented the use of its trackbed south of Plym Bridge as originally envisaged. An independent parallel alignment had to be found for the new 7'0¼" gauge railway and another level crossing was required, this time mid-way between Plym Bridge and Marsh Mills; once again, the 4'6" gauge line, being the first on the scene, had a right of way; minor diversions to the Cann Quarry Branch and the canal were necessary.

The wooden trestle bridge across Plym Bridge Road, at the foot of the Cann Wood Incline, with the Launceston line's bridge further along the road.
(Photograph - F.H.C. Casbourn, courtesy of the Stephenson Locomotive Society)

Wranglings on the Tavistock Line

In 1846, the London & South Western Railway, which at that time reached no further west than Basingstoke, bought the isolated Bodmin & Wadebridge Railway as notice of its intention to move into the West Country. It already had designs on Plymouth and no doubt encouraged the concern of the day that for reasons of national security, London should be linked to all strategic ports and naval bases by railways of a common gauge. This could not be achieved using the 7'0¼" gauge and the South Devon Railway was reluctant to lay 4'8½" on its main line into Plymouth, as it would benefit rival companies.

A train of china-clay (in casks) at the foot of the Cann Wood Incline, having just crossed the trestle bridge across Plym Bridge Road.
(Photograph - F.H.C. Casbourn, courtesy of the Stephenson Locomotive Society)

There were successive delays in the choice between waiting for the London & South Western Railway, still 160 miles away, and authorising a 7'0¼" line much sooner. The latter won the day, but not without the South Devon & Tavistock Railway having to concede to the condition that were a 4'8½" line ever to make a connection with its own, the Company would have to make the necessary arrangements to accommodate 4'8½" gauge trains. It would have preferred to fight this ruling, but the wranglings had festered too long at the expense of time and money. The Bill was passed on July 24th, 1854, and the heavily engineered line was opened on June 21st, 1859, at least five years later than might otherwise have occurred.

It may be of interest to mention that the London & South Western Railway finally reached the area at Lidford (as it was then spelt) and exercised the agreement to have a third rail added to the South Devon's line down to Plymouth, to permit the working of 4'8½" gauge trains via the Plym Valley. This was completed on May 17th, 1876 and for the next 16 years (until the total abolition of the 7'0¼" gauge), trains of three gauges could be seen at the crossing of the two lines, between Plym Bridge and Marsh Mills and again at Laira.

Lee Moor Crossing, looking towards Marsh Mills, in about 1922.
(Photograph - F.H.C. Casbourn, courtesy of the Stephenson Locomotive Society)

The Lee Moor Tramway Termini

Lee Moor China-Clay Works, the marshalling point for Plymouth-bound trains, was at Torycombe, about ½ mile south-west of Lee Moor village. The Torycombe Incline took the Tramway up from the works to the village, from where it continued in a generally eastern direction to the ultimate terminus at the clay works at Cholwich Town, just east of the old route of the Yelverton - Ivybridge road. At the top of the incline, there was a branch to the Dartmoor China-Clay Works at Wotter.

The original and replacement Torycombe Inclines had nearby upper termini, though facing different directions. As originally constructed in 1854, it ascended from the middle of Lee Moor China-Clay Works, but the replacement took an easier gradient from the west end, with the lines serving the China-Clay and brickworks on a branch terminating at the brickworks.

The Cholwich Town extension opened with the original Torycombe Incline in 1853 and closed in about 1933, although one source dates this as early as 1910. The Wotter Branch opened in 1855 and closed in 1900, save for a short stub into a stone quarry near the incline summit, which survived until sometime between 1936 and 1939; the quarry's eventual closure rendered the Torycombe Incline redundant.

The Route of the Tramway

Trains leaving Torycombe for Plymouth immediately crossed Wotter Brook beyond the throat of the sidings. Initially, this was bridged by the Lower Leigh Viaduct, 627ft long and 70ft at its maximum height. This dated from 1854, but needed remedial attention to match the standard of the reconstructed line of 1858. Evidently the repair was not satisfactory as it was closed in 1878, the line being diverted around the side of the valley on the "Wotter Curve" to make an easier upstream crossing of the Brook. Leaving the Wotter valley, the route entered a long cutting crossed by a minor road on Truelove Bridge, soon followed by Whitegates Level Crossing on the Yelverton-Plympton road.

After passing north of the ancient earthwork of Boringdon Camp, the Tramway reached the top of the Cann Wood Incline. Over a length of 1¼ miles and on an average gradient of 1 in 11, this dropped the trains from 380ft to 40ft at Plym Bridge, the end of the Lee Moor Tramway proper.

Below Plym Bridge, the trains used the tracks of the Plymouth & Dartmoor Railway's Cann Quarry Branch, which followed the Cann Quarry Canal as far as Marsh Mills and then turned west to cross the River Plym on a two span cast-iron bridge; at the east end of the bridge was a weighbridge cottage which marked the junction with the Plymouth & Dartmoor Railway's dismantled Plympton Branch.

The two span bridge across the River Plym and the Weighbridge Cottage, a scene little changed to this day.
(Photograph - R.T. Coxon)

The route then ran along the north side of the main turnpike road into Plymouth which it crossed at Crabtree, just after joining the Plymouth & Dartmoor Railway's Princetown Line. It remained on the south side of the turnpike to Laira where it turned south-west to cross the South Devon main line on the famous level crossing. Tramway movements were protected by the main line company; in later years there was a standard Great Western signal at each end of the crossing, controlled by Laira Junction Signal Box.

Untouched "Lee Moor No.1" and partially-restored "Lee Moor No.2" seen on May 18th, 1966, when they had ventured outside of Torycombe Shed for the first time in over 20 years.
(Photograph - E.R. Shepherd)

South of the crossing, the route passed through Laira Yard (now occupied by the stabling area for Inter-City 125 train sets), where there was a siding to tranship the china-clay to main line wagons, and then on to the present-day road junction between Embankment Road and Hele's Terrace, near the Western National bus depôt, where the Plymouth & Dartmoor Railway continued to Sutton Harbour. At this point, the Lee Moor Tramway trains used the Plymouth & Dartmoor Railway's branch to Martin's Wharf, a few yards downstream from Laira Road Bridge.

When Lee Moor Tramway trains commenced, the Plymouth & Dartmoor Railway and the South Devon Railway's 7'0¼" gauge track to Sutton Harbour were the only lines to penetrate this area. There was much subsequent railway development, and the juxtaposition of the various railways is best unravelled by reference to John Gillham's well-known large scale map.

Working the Tramway

The operation of the Tramway was complicated by the presence of the two inclines. They were worked on the counterbalance principle, the descending trains being heavier than those ascending, avoiding the need for a winding engine. Speed was regulated by band brakes on the winding drums to which the cables were attached. The drum houses were at the summits, where they were situated under a double track section on which wagons were marshalled before or after their passage of the incline.

The level crossing of the A38 at Crabtree on June 11th, 1955. The solitary car, bound for Plymouth, is a stark contrast to the three-lane dual carriageway, roundabout and multi-million pound flyover that dominates this scene today.
(Photograph - E.R. Shepherd)

Both inclines had half-way passing loops. These had self-acting points at their lower ends so that a descending train would leave them set correctly for the next ascending train. Below the passing loops, the running lines were single track, and above were 3-rail with a common centre one. The self-acting points on the Cann Wood Incline later proved unsatisfactory and were replaced by two tracks which were interlaced to avoid widening the bridge at the bottom.

On the 1 in 7 Torycombe Incline, trains were generally limited to two wagons. The descending train had to be several tons heavier to overcome the weight of the incline rope and the various friction losses, and some 4 ton water tank wagons could be used to increase the weight of descending trains; they would discharge their contents before returning to the top of the incline. The Cann Wood Incline was no steeper than 1 in 11, and up to six wagons could be despatched together. The payload of one wagon was about 5 tons of clay, so the need for water ballast wagons did not arise.

The winding drums on the Cann Wood Incline were offset from each other and connected by simple gears, so that they revolved in opposite directions. The two cables came off the top of the drums so that as one cable was wound in, the other unwound. Each cable passed up through rollers in the Drum House floor to connect with the wagons. On the Torycombe Incline, there was only one drum with a central dividing piece, one cable coming from the top of its half and the other coming off the bottom of its half, thus achieving the same operation.

Apart from on the section between Torycombe and the top of the Cann Wood Incline, trains were horse-drawn. They were generally limited to a maximum of five wagons and drawn by a pair of horses. On a typical day, each of the seven pairs of horses might make two return trips to take about 400 tons of clay down the Tramway. 14 horses were stabled at Lee Moor, just above the Public Hall, and another 14, used on the section below Plym Bridge, were stabled at Martin's Wharf.

The wagons were much smaller than those of a main line railway. An early batch was constructed by Charles Roberts & Co. of Wakefield, but subsequent examples were built at Lee Moor. Most were four-wheel trucks with a 4'3" wheelbase and dumb (i.e. unsprung) buffers. They had a central drawbar for coupling to the incline cable and side chains for horse haulage. The total fleet eventually numbered about 140.

The End of the Plymouth & Dartmoor Railway

The Plymouth & Dartmoor Railway continued to operate for another 25 years. In 1883, the Princetown end was replaced by the 4'8½" gauge Princetown Railway, which used most of the trackbed between Princetown and Dousland and then made a connection with the Tavistock line at Yelverton. The remaining section was left in place until about 1916, but was probably moribund between Dousland and Crabtree in or soon after 1883; it was certainly disused in 1907, as a writer in the "Railway Magazine" reported that he had encountered a landslip, and several wire fences and gates across the line.

The Plymouth & Dartmoor remained in being and obtained the Act of Parliament for the London & South Western Railway to advance into the South Hams rural area to the south-east of Plymouth. It finally passed away in 1921.

Introduction of Steam Locomotives

Expanding production at Lee Moor resulted in greater tonnages passing along the Tramway and to increase its capacity, two 0-4-0 saddle tank locomotives were ordered from Peckett & Sons Ltd of Bristol. To prepare the Tramway for locomotive operation, the section between Torycombe and the top of the Cann Wood Incline was relaid with sleepered track, and an engine shed was built at Torycombe. In 1907 or 1908, the level crossing at Whitegates was protected with gates and signals. The signals were operated by wires anchored to brackets on the gates in such a way that they were cleared when the gates were set for trains to cross.

Both locomotives carried names, originally painted on the water saddle, but later replaced by brass plates in the same position. "Lee Moor No.1", works number 783 was delivered on March 24th, 1899 and "Lee Moor No.2", works number 784, followed on April 6th. They were standard gauge Peckett "M4" class, but with wide tyres to allow the wheel flanges to be set in for the 4'6" gauge.

Principal dimensions were: length 18'8"; width 7'0:; height 10'4"; weight including 2 tons of coal carried in a bunker inside the cab 13 tons 15 cwt; wheel diameter 2' 6"; wheelbase 5'0"; two outside cylinders 10" x 14"; working pressure 140 lb/sq. in. (nominal) and 120 lb/sq.in. (working); tractive effort (at working pressure) 6,800 lbs. Both locomotives carried a lifting jack with traverser on the running plate, so that the crew could rerail the train without calling for assistance!

The first driver was Fred Andrews, an ex-Great Western man who worked the Lee Moor engines for 12 years. Other drivers were Edgar Quest, Fred Alford and, latterly, George Poynter. Firemen included Bob Brooks and Erne Cox. The crews soon found the open backs to the cab rather exposed and rather ungainly detachable shrouds were constructed at Lee Moor.

Initially, one locomotive was in use at a time, but as traffic increased, one spent the day shunting at Torycombe, whilst the other made the 3 mile round trip working to the top of Cann Wood Incline; the journey time from Lee Moor Brick Works to Cann Wood was 8-9

Laira Crossing, seen from Embankment Road in about 1922, with china-clay train bound for Plymouth.
(Photograph - F.H.C. Casbourn, courtesy of the Stephenson Locomotive Society)

A train of empties for Lee Moor, passes through Laira Yard in about 1922. Compare the diminutive Tramway wagons with those behind. This area now accommodates stabling sidings for Inter-City 125 train sets.
(Photograph - F.H.C. Casbourn, courtesy of the Stephenson Locomotive Society)

minutes. The loaded clay was generally bulked into two daily trains up to a maximum of about 45 wagons each. The locomotives could haul much greater loads, but china-clay is extremely slippery, especially on rails, so adhesion and braking capability were the limiting factors. The record load was attributed to Fred Alford who, with the advantage of a start from the brickworks and by not stopping at Torycombe Level Crossing, successfully took 50 wagons over the summit in Truelove Cutting and then on to Cann Wood.

The locomotives could have been used to greater advantage had they also been employed on the lower section, from the foot of the Cann Wood Incline into Plymouth. However, the Great Western Railway, which at that time operated the railways adjacent to the 4'6" gauge, prevented this by refusing to alter the agreement that allowed only horse-drawn traffic the right to across its lines. When the Lee Moor Tramway trains were introduced, there was only one track to cross - at Laira, but subsequent development increased this number to four, plus a crossing of the London and South Western Railway's Cattewater Goods Branch near Laira Bridge. Locomotive haulage along so many fragmented sections between these various crossings was clearly unworkable.

The Great Western Railway's stance was understandable, as the expense of maintaining these various crossings was its responsibility. Furthermore, it was eager to carry the china-clay traffic and was not about to alter the crossing conditions so that they would favour the continued use of the 4'6" gauge. When the Lee Moor Tramway was opened, it had been intended to make a connection at Plym Bridge, initially with transhipment, but ultimately with the Tramway re-gauged to permit through running.

The clay company realised that it would not have been in its interest to undertake this; it would have lost control of the running of its trains and would have been subject to the conveyance charges imposed by the Great Western. Despite the different gauge and horse-haulage, the status quo was the attractive alternative and the Lee Moor Tramway retained the 4'6" gauge throughout its life.

Casks of china-clay being transferred from Lee Moor Tramway wagons on Martin's Wharf in the 1930's. The original Laira Road Bridge, replaced in October 1961, and the parapet of the Turnchapel Branch railway bridge can be seen in the background.
(Photograph - A Bray, courtesy of M.E.J. Dart)

The Tramway's Limitations leading to Final Closure

As production at Lee Moor increased, the shortcomings of the Tramway were exposed. The unusual gauge was not as great an impediment as might have been supposed, as most of the traffic was self-contained; the bulk of it was the china-clay being taken to the quayside at Martin's Wharf.

To ease the load on the Tramway, a pipe line was constructed to take the china-clay in slurry form to the works at Marsh Mills for treatment and drying, and was brought into use in 1927. From there, the china-clay could be taken by the Great Western Railway, and with the advantage of the standard gauge, it could be conveyed to better port facilities at Fowey in Cornwall. The Tramway continued to convey clay, however, and the two engines were overhauled in the 1930's.

"Lee Moor No. 2" was seen returning to Torycombe with 17 empty wagons in August 1939, but during the war years, only a skeleton service was run; this included the movement of stores originating from the H.M. Dockyard at Devonport. In March 1944, a visitor found the two locomotives locked in their shed and no traffic moving, but some wagons were loaded and the rails showed signs of recent use. In July 1945, a permanent-way gang was seen attending to the track near Plym Bridge, and the March/April 1946 issue of the bi-monthly "Railway Magazine" reported that the Tramway "reopened on October 8th, 1945".

George Poynter stated that the last occasion an engine was used, was when he worked "Lee Moor No.2" on December 31st, 1945. Another employee recalls the line in a state of disuse in early 1946, and a visitor to the Tramway on March 3rd, 1947, found the rails in the woods near Wotter Curve covered with a thick layer of fallen leaves. Precise closure dates of industrial lines are notoriously difficult to confirm, but these recollections by various observers suggest that hitherto reported closure dates in 1946 or 1947 are wrong.

After 1945, a short section was kept open for the conveyance of sand between Marsh Mills and Maddock's Concrete Works just south of Laira Yard. This was solely to preserve the right to cross the Great Western Railway's main line at Laira, as the possibility of using the Tramway to transport china-clay by-products and in particular gravel, was being considered. However, the presence of the Cann Wood Incline and the other peculiar features of the line did not make its further use a viable proposition.

The decision having been made to close it, the traffic to Maddocks Concrete Works was taken off the Tramway. The last recorded working at Laira Junction was on August 26th, 1960, when wagons bound for the concrete works crossed at 11.19am and returned, empty, at 1.27pm; the famous crossing over the main line was removed in October of the same year.

During these twilight years, the two locomotives had remained in their shed at Torycombe and all the wagons were left to the mercy of the elements at various points along the Tramway. In 1955 for example, there were 34 in Laira Sidings, 7 in Marsh Mills Sidings, 22 on the main running line near Wotter Curve, 8 at Torycombe and a number hidden in Lee Moor Brickworks Sidings. In 1961, all the wagons still on the Tramway were scrapped and the rails down to Plym Bridge were lifted, so that a second pipeline from Lee Moor could be laid along the trackbed.

A derelict wagon outside Torycombe Engine Shed in August 1955, when the Tramway above Marsh Mills had been closed for nearly 10 years. The two locomotives were inside the shed, facing, at that time, an uncertain future.
(Photograph - M.E.J. Dart)

"Lee Moor No.2" and the rebuilt wagon
outside Torycombe Engine Shed in July 1970.
(Photograph from the R.E. Taylor collection)

Restoration at Torycombe

Fortuitously, the fate of the locomotives had not been decided and if the truth were known, there was probably no one in the Clay Company prepared to undertake the dastardly deed of selling them to a breaker. The plight of the two forlorn engines did not escape the attention of local railway enthusiasts and after discussions with the Clay Company, the possibility of saving one or both of them was raised at the 1963 Annual General Meeting of the Plymouth Railway Circle.

The Circle was formed in 1948 as a general railway interest group, holding meetings on alternate Monday evenings in the Mutley area of Plymouth, as it still does to this day. There was no provision for preservation in its aims, so a separate "Lee Moor Tramway Preservation Society" was formed in February 1964.

A restoration programme was discussed with the Clay Company and the first working party made a start in May 1964. Although the locomotives had been locked away for many years, the shed was showing signs of neglect and was no longer weatherproof. It was subject to regular flooding and the smoke ventilator immediately above "Lee Moor No.1" was leaking. The shed had no electricity and was found with broken cupboards, an accumulation of rubbish and an inspection pit partly filled with china-clay.

The first year was spent putting the shed in order, to serve its dual purpose as a workshop and museum. With no mains drainage nearby, the risk of further flooding was alleviated by constructing a stone-filled soakaway around the perimeter. The roof was repaired, the walls whitewashed and electricity installed. The shed was built specifically for the two engines, so there was little spare room inside the building. To create space for working parties and to permit the positioning of the locomotives for photography, a short length of track was reinstated outside the shed.

"Lee Moor No.1" was in the worse state because of her position under the leaking ventilator, and some of her motion had been dismantled. Apart from being given a liberal coating of old engine oil to prevent further deterioration, she was left untouched whilst the main effort was directed towards renovating her sister.

"Lee Moor No.2" had been in use until the end of locomotive working and underneath the grime, she was found to be in much better condition, and complete, except for one of the two brass works plates. During the period from 1965 to 1970, she was cleaned down to bare metal, rust proofed, repainted and relined. The missing works plate was replaced by a replica cast from the surviving original. The original eventually turned up in a display cabinet at the National Railway Museum in York, but no one has established the circumstances surrounding its arrival.

A number of exhibits relating to the Tramway and other local lines were displayed on the inside walls of the shed, and one of the signals which protected the Tramway from the main line trains at Laira was put into working order and erected.

The locomotives alone could not create a complete exhibit without one of the Tramway's china-clay wagons. All those left abandoned at various points along the line had been scrapped, but one had languished in a stream since being derailed in an incident on the Cann Wood Incline in the 1930's. The Clay Company retrieved it for the Society and parked it in the engine shed; "Lee Moor No.1" had her buffers and couplings removed, so that she could be moved forward to make room for the new arrival. After 30 years exposure to the elements,

A precarious moment at Saltram on July 20th, 1970, as "Lee Moor No.2" is swung over the pond and fence towards the coach house.
(Photograph - B. Mills)

none of the wagon's timber could be salvaged, so a complete rebuild was undertaken, using new wood, the ironwork that had been recovered and odds and ends found at Lee Moor.

In 1969, work on "Lee Moor No.2" and the wagon had reached the stage where they could make their first journey as a complete train - on to the short length of track outside the shed! The result of the hard work put into the restoration could be seen.

The Future of the Project

It had always been realised that the engine shed was not an ideal home for the exhibits. The hostile Dartmoor climate continued to produce running condensation, despite the repairs that had been undertaken on the building. Furthermore, its location was not in a tourist area, so the only people who would see this important reminder of the area's industrial past would be those who made a specific visit.

As occasionally happens, an unrelated event proved to be the catalyst for a solution. In 1969, details of a Steam Engine Rally to be held in Chelson Meadow near Saltram in July 1970, were circulated to interested parties, including the Lee Moor Tramway Preservation Society. The Society saw the publicity value of displaying "Lee Moor No. 2" and the wagon at the event on a low-loader. The Clay Company offered to provide transport, and this provided the fillip to complete the restoration work in time for the rally.

The event was looked upon as a weekend outing for the engine and wagon, but at least one Member was considering a long term plan for the Collection. A museum had been created in the National Trust's Penrhyn Castle in North Wales, which originally belonged to the owner of the local slate quarries and their associated railway system. The circumstances in respect of the Lee Moor china-clay workings, the Tramway and the Morley family's home at Saltram House, now in the care of the National Trust, were identical.

With Penrhyn as a precedent, English China Clays and the Lee Moor Tramway Preservation Society approached the National Trust, which agreed to house the Collection in the coach house at Saltram. Arrangements were made at such short notice that the engine and wagon were able to go direct from the Chelson Meadow rally to Saltram, where they arrived on Monday July 20th, 1970.

There was no direct access to the coach house, so the wagon and then the locomotive had to be swung over a pond by crane and then winched and pushed on steel plates over the cobbled courtyard, a difficult seven hour operation; "Lee Moor No.2" was lined up in front of the wagon on August 5th. The premises were ideal, especially as the presence of tenants in flats over the courtyard made it very difficult for uninvited visitors to approach the area undetected. However, the only way into the coach house was through a private gate and past the pond, so opening to the public had to await the construction of a new entrance direct from the courtyard.

The Museum was eventually opened to the public on May 28th, 1978, initially on Sunday afternoons only, when a steward was in attendance. An altar-rail barrier was subsequently erected, which allowed the access hours to be harmonised with those of Saltram House itself.

To return to 1970, sister engine "Lee Moor No.1" remained in the shed at Torycombe after the departure of "Lee Moor No.2" and the wagon. English China Clays was planning its own museum covering the china-clay industry and it asked the Society to undertake the restoration of "Lee Moor No.1" for exhibition. In return, the ownership of "Lee Moor No.2" would be transferred to the Society.

The Lee Moor Tramway Preservation Society had been formed in 1964 specifically to restore the locomotives at Torycombe. With the completion of its aims within sight and with the agreement of both Memberships, the Society was absorbed back into the Plymouth Railway Circle on April 1st, 1974. Now under the guise of the Plymouth Railway Circle, the restoration of "Lee Moor No.1" was completed on November 20th, 1974 and she was transported to the Wheal Martyn China Clay Museum near St Austell on March 17th 1975, in time for the official opening.

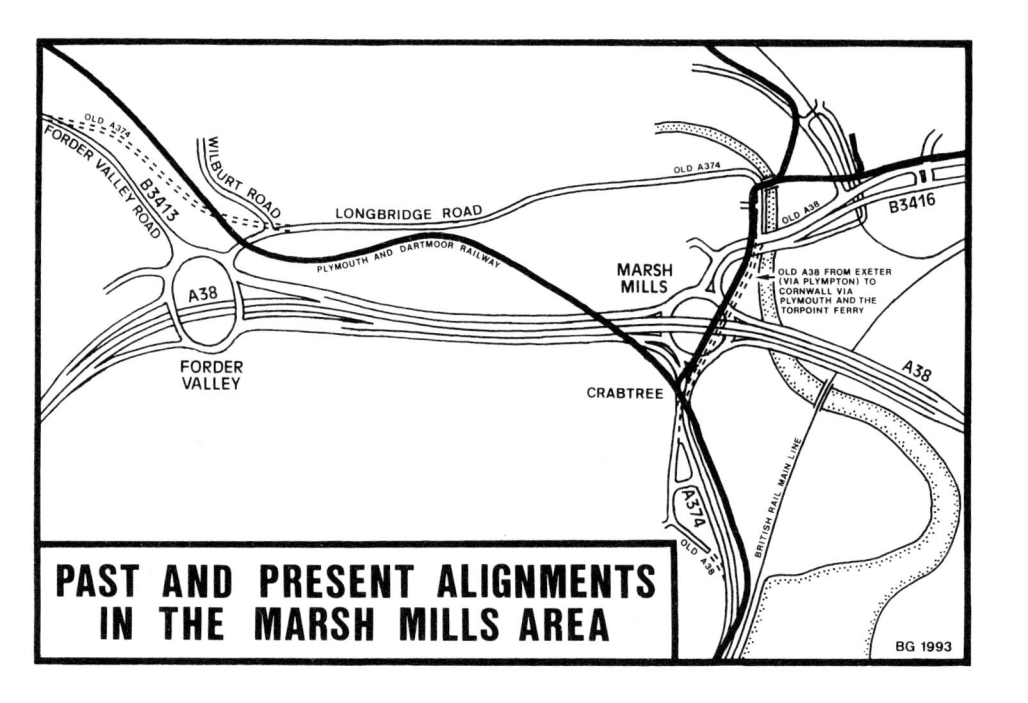

PAST AND PRESENT ALIGNMENTS IN THE MARSH MILLS AREA

Present Day Remains
(With Ordnance Survey Grid References)

A new road, by-passing the villages of Wotter and Lee Moor, cuts through the second Torycombe Incline, which can be seen behind the bus shelter (SX 568615) just west of the junction with the old road climbing up from Torycombe. Torycombe Engine Shed (SX 565611) survives at Lee Moor China-Clay Works and although on private property, is within sight of the Plympton - Lee Moor Village road. There is no public access to any part of the Tramway, but the trackbed can be seen from Truelove Bridge (SX 549606) and again at Whitegates Crossing (SX 546602), where the gate posts (but not the gates) remain; the profile of the trackbed across the road is still evident, especially to speeding motorists!

The next vantage point is at Plym Bridge, where the bottom of the Cann Wood Incline crossed the Plympton - Plym Bridge road. The present-day bridge (SX 524586) dates from December 1961 and is narrower than the original, built purely to carry the second pipeline laid after the Tramway was dismantled. Where the incline levels out, there are ruinous buildings which were the stables for the horses working the lower section of the Tramway. Some disturbed lengths of rail hereabouts, mark the junction of the Plymouth and Dartmoor Railway's Cann Quarry branch and the end of the Lee Moor Tramway proper (SX 522585).

The section from Plym Bridge to Coypool Road at Marsh Mills, is now part of the Cyclebag/Sustainable Transport Limited path and cycle route from Goodameavy to Laira Bridge, and whilst all evidence of the Tramway has been buried, the actual route is used.

The only substantial length of track still in situ is from Coypool Road to the River Plym. Most is out of sight under dense undergrowth in a shallow cutting on the south side of a footpath, but it emerges to cross the two-span bridge over the Plym (SX 520568). A stone wall has been built over the track at both ends of the bridge as part of a flood-prevention scheme. It is still watched over by the weighbridge cottage, creating a remarkably complete scene in an area which has seen so much change in recent years.

The rest of the route into Plymouth has been obliterated by road works and British Rail development. Where the two 4'6" gauge lines once converged (SX 516566), road vehicles from Plymouth join the Marsh Mills Roundabout under the elevated section of the A38 trunk road. The level crossing over the Cattewater Goods Branch (SX 500544) can be seen from Laira Road Bridge and Martin's Quay (SX 500542) survives; however the railway buildings were demolished in October 1992 when the former scrapyard was redeveloped as a boat storage area.

Although not relevant to the Lee Moor Tramway, it is worth mentioning that there are widespread remains of the original Plymouth and Dartmoor Railway. The 620 yard Leigham Tunnel of 1823, although boarded up, is well preserved and the northern portal (SX 514586) is alongside the Leigham - Plym Bridge Road. There are long sections of undisturbed trackbed, particularly in Holt Wood and again across Roborough Down, where most of the cylindrical granite mileposts are still in place. The stables where the horses were changed, still stand near Clearbrook (SX 517651) over a century after they ceased to serve their original purpose. Despite its early closure, a substantial length of the trackbed of the Plympton Branch survives as a raised pavement on the north side of Plymouth Road, eastward from the junction with Larkham Lane (SX 529566).

Thanks to the dedication and foresight of those enthusiasts who formed the Lee Moor Tramway Preservation Society and the invaluable support of English China Clays and the National Trust, both locomotives have been saved, and the last surviving wagon has been restored from dereliction. So whilst modern development continues to erode evidence of the 4'6" gauge system, a tangible reminder has been preserved.

The Plymouth Railway Circle arranges occasional conducted walks along various sections of the old trackbeds, often with permission to cover lengths now in private ownership. Participants, who do not necessarily have to be Circle Members, have the advantage of a guide who will point out the remains.